My Body Bonded With Super Glue

Lisa Tellor-Kelley

Advance Praise for *My Body Bonded With Super Glue*

"In *My Body Bonded With Super Glue*, Lisa Tellor-Kelley writes memorably of her battle with breast cancer. In "When a Sparrow Thinks Like An Eagle," she characterizes cancer as the predator and herself as the sparrow that attacks back with fury. Elsewhere she refers to herself as well as other women engaged in the fight: "We are a new type of gladiator," she writes. "We have been / to the spring, filled our empty mouths / with *I am*." As she embarks upon life after cancer, she finds strength in the "wild flame" of her resilient body. "I shake my silver bracelets," she writes, inspiring others to join her dance."
—Allison Funk, author of *The Visible Woman*

""I pray / an exalted crane will sing / lessons of survivors"—Lisa Tellor-Kelley's chapbook *is* that crane. These poems sing lessons, sure, as well as songs of loss and pain and love and grace. This work is grounded in the physical body—breasts, tumors, scars, tongues, thighs, nipples, skin, and sternum—even as the poems transport us well beyond the literal, thanks to Tellor-Kelley's ingenious, rollicking use of figurative language."
—Valerie Vogrin, author of *Things We'll Need for the Coming Difficulties* (Willow Springs Press)

My Body
Bonded
With
Super Glue

poems by

Lisa Tellor-Kelley

Copyright © 2021 Lisa Tellor-Kelley

All Rights Reserved. This book or any portion thereof may not be reproduced, in whole or in part, in any form (beyond that permitted by Sections 107 and 108 of the U.S Copyright Law and except by reviewers for the public press), without the express written permission of the publisher except for the use of brief quotations in a book review.

Tellor-Kelly/Lisa, author

My Body Bonded With Super Glue / Lisa Tellor-Kelley

Poems

ISBN: 978-1-7365167-1-3

Edited by: Beth Gordon
Book Design: Amanda McLeod
Cover Art: Deirdre Burnside
Cover Design: Amanda McLeod

PUBLISHER
Animal Heart Press
P.O. Box 322
Thetford Center, Vermont 05075
www.animalheartpress.net

for Jeff

Table of Contents

DIAGNOSIS 9
    Girl in Chemise 10
    Bra Beginnings 11
    18,000 Folds Close Heaven Gates 12
    Eviction 13
    A Warm, Widespread Panic 14
    Breaking Up Is Hard to Do 15
    Sternum Against Stone 16
    Moving Left on the Number Line 17
    Skin Jacketing His Paper Doll 18
    A Poet's Prescription 19

POST-OP 21
    I Suggest Healing to a Bollywood Beat 22
    We Are Born Again 23
    Repatterning Body and Mind 24
    My Reflection In Black Satin 25
    When A Sparrow Thinks Like An Eagle 26
    Pray & Push A Red Devil 27
    Tequila Shots and Bullet Proof Vests 28
    Meridian Road 29
    Binding Wounds With Pink Ribbon 30

EVOLUTION 31
    My Body Bonded With Super Glue 32
    A Controlled Burn With a Twist of Lime 33
    Peeled Bark and Blushing Thighs 34
    Cupping Coffee 35

Chasing Ghost in Corkscrew Swamp While Smoking Lemon Bean 36
Thrilled by the Burn 37
Boys Who Wear White Enjoy Eating Red 38
Life's Self Inflicted Performance 39
Amid A Body's Civil War 40
An Ant's Exploration 41
Praise a Confident Woman 42

Acknowledgements 45

About the Author 47

DIAGNOSIS

Girl in Chemise

Art is a lie that makes us realize the truth- Pablo Picasso

I was given a choice:
remove one, or two breasts. I wanted to
remain whole, no half or void look. I wanted to
have connection without the disconnect. I wanted to
feel the softness of lips on my nipples. I wanted two
plump pieces of flesh against my palms. I wanted to
feel numb because I was fragile and broken.
Forced to make an artist's decision. To

decide as Picasso would have:
will the subject's breasts be distorted,
disproportionate, discolored? Blue-gray

chemise hangs upon a slender torso, only
one breast visible, admits to wanting
sexual desire. And me wanting

the natural number two.

Bra Beginnings

I vividly remember my first cotton bra. I was a 13-year-old
middle school graduate. I was self-conscious
as the carbon dioxide rose in the flour
sifted mounds on my chest. They empowered me
to kiss boys with my mouth open. I was eager
to wrap my small, perfect patty cakes
in soft cups of push-up cotton. Bras

were increasingly sexy as I advanced
in high school. A pearl
white bra was not cool. I was dead
jealous of red & pink hearts,
polka dot prints, or hot pink triangles
with intimate lace straps. An unfilled teen bra
dream.

I am 35
years older. I now research
how a single cell makes a meal
of estrogen, becomes pleasantly plump,
multiples, mutates and pierces
abalone armor, leaving me soft,
empty cotton cups
and my lover's mouth
an empty tomb.

18,000 Folds Close Heaven Gates

At forty-nine I felt soft
massive explosions, nothing like a cherry
blossom. They unfolded inside my breasts
and I learned to bend. Inside, small

lumps formed beneath my supple rose
petal skin; I never appreciated
God's foxglove as beautiful,
yet intoxicatingly deadly. I knew
I had to become flexible, remain growing
and never break. At the beginning

my friends folded pieces of paper. Composed messages
in each crinkle and bend; a pulpwood molded Lord
Crane to fulfill my wish: she would not
carry me to heaven. Bending me

was not an easy task. Folding skin
into 18,000 sharp, crisp, folds
was tedious, precise work. My lotuses
were created by a skin origami
Grandmaster, using math equations
to secure a new animated bouquet
on my chest.

Eviction

I feel I housed
Big Time Charlie
in my body,
and I no longer
have the need
to open my eyes
each morning
and welcome life.
I want to strip
my mind, numb
my body and
prepare to evict. Charlie,
he only wants parts
I want. So I discard
those parts. The vase
that holds my spirit
is disfigured. Two
straight white cracks

across my breast. Nothing
replaces the feel
of ice-cold breezes
as they blow across
hot pink flesh,
commanding them
to come forth
as Christ called
Lazarus. My lover

is an artist
of love-making
and never allows
Big Time Charlie's paintbrush
to stain my frosted vase
colors of gray and black.

A Warm, Widespread Panic

It's 5:30 am and still
pitch black outside the window
in my bedroom. My husband and I
should be on the road. We are late.

I shower in a warm, widespread panic,
my fears rein in my brain, on high alert. I am a child
playing hide and seek between hard water
rain droplets. A secret Sibyl whispers,
*It is going to be
okay.* My life in Dr. Aft's hands is good,
but nothing about it feels good
this morning. When I arrive,
I am supposed to change

into an oversized gown, paper hat
and purple no-skid socks. I take off
my clothing and change into my surgical
wardrobe. I feel the soft cotton gown
lightly touch my breasts. My hands
cup each breast and I pray

an exalted crane will sing
lessons of survivors. Coax me to tilt
my face towards the incandescent
sun, face flush with rage and rejoice
that the mutilation will be minimal. I am told
there will always be unexpected encounters
in Eden. Sharp twists or curves, like kinks
in a garden hose.

Breaking Up Is Hard to Do

It is natural to dislike saying good-bye
to my breasts. Their beauty, vibrancy and fun are preserved
in my mind. Of course, some qualities will be destroyed.

Yet, I refuse to let go. I will not
let this diseased anatomy be forced upon me. My breast
is being denied an organic end, and yet I know
the dead will be reanimated. It is hard to stop struggling,

let the end happen, and to go to my prayer closet
and grieve. Let searing waves of sadness quench my thirst,
let the pain that seems unlivable, become reality. I will stay
and wait for something unexpectedly comforting. Letting go

is a delicate art, holding on
is at odds with releasing.

Sternum Against Stone

A green and black cat's eye, the entrance opens
into the earth. My jump sends me tumbling
down the shaft, sunlight stirs up

the swallows. They revolve clockwise. Counter
I drop through the rising column
of beating wings

thwacking against my empty chest. I have
recently become familiar with mazes
of mad plumbing, doglegged down

through thick layers of limestone beneath
wood ridges, pockets of holes. This subterranean world has

limitless possibilities. I wrestle through
the cave, encounter a boulder's squeeze and I am able

to slide between the tight blackness,
sternum against stone. A new experience-
impenetrable darkness. On the surface,
light comes from starlight, moonlight, fire.

Light! I adjust my eyes,
as darkness weighs heavy.

Moving Left on the Number Line

I have to consider a negative number; I know
for every real number there exists its opposite. So there

will be something more than nothing? Good!
The number zero is neither negative, nor positive,

when my natural number two is removed,
the remainder is empty, horizontal hatch marks. A doctor adds

two back to the number zero and I will be a whole,
a common, ordinal number. My number two will be real,

positive, and complex. There is divisibility
by the number two, and I will not include zero

in my natural numbers. I want two
dainty roses made from the supple marble of my body.

Skin Jacketing His Paper Doll

He looks intensely,
like a child ready to cut
and play with his paper
doll. He shaves and shapes
along a thin dotted line
made with his black felt tip
Sharpie. A guide for his scissors
to slice away corruption, leaving a spider
white marble skin jacket. He never denies,
my lines will be made from smoke
and mirrors. He presents a Charm-

Tex blue hospital gown, minus two
paper folding tabs to bend over my shoulders
to conceal my petite princesses. I stand poised,
motionless and make myself Flat
Stanley. A doctor removes my tissue dress
and begins discussing the trends
used to complement my negative space:
two white lines, minus my pointed cones
and my standard half dollar size circles,
in a subtle shade of red.

A Poet's Prescription

A poet's medicine is a pink sun
setting, reposed around a surfboard
table loaded with witches, herbalists and ghost
busters who love words
and enjoy the tastes of red and black
caviar, sushi, raw oysters. Indulgent foods
make all mouths open heavy awaiting to receive
strawberries dripping in spicy chocolate
fondue, speak of the pricey
ice wine and hashish, smoked
meats and imported beers; I recommend

as poets we munch, drink, discuss the emotional
stress of a void chest and how satin slides across
a physician's tongue during a Red Devil cocktail. We force ourselves
to vomit up pages filled with teeth and knuckles, scratch
our emotions into paper, rub images into readers' minds
and explain the family recipes of how meat is removed, scored
and decisions are made whether to rub the cuts with sugar or salt.

POST-OP

I Suggest Healing to a Bollywood Beat

A Bollywood beat pumps
in my head. I shake my silver
bracelets and dance with women
who are absent of breasts. I lead
women towards marsala tunes. Music
makes the body melt into
unrestricted movements. Allowing access
to parts denied and disowned. Once afraid,
I find courage through movement.

It has taken me eight years to drift
into my blue velvet space and become
an exotic creature. Without my breasts
I feel the need to dance with purpose
and remind the world I carry
a provocative blank canvas.

I dance to celebrate two
scissored white, straight lines.
I dance to celebrate beautiful breasts
that tried to kill me.
I dance to fast, two-rhythm thumps,
heartbeats, until resumption.
I dance to celebrate the absence of my flesh.

We Are Born Again

We are a new type of gladiator. We wear armor
made of pink cauliflower coral, Caribbean pearls,
and rosy feather stars. Our ruby tongues
cut words of truth from the soft undersides
of our bosoms. We wear soft breast-plated armor. Like an eagle
we see clearly through frozen water. We have been
to the spring, filled our empty mouths
with *I am* and emerged as Granite
City steel. Shared pools of molten metal. Our chests
adorn two white scars drawn in our sand
colored skin. We are Esther's women

revealing a body's conspiracy. Perfectly round pearls
form words and our lips release the fires
from our lungs while we feel the Devil
still nipping, silently, at our toes.

Repatterning Body and Mind

My husband wants me
to lay still as he gently kisses my breasts
each night. He helps me absorb
every sensation. I memorize
each piece of skin-to-skin contact: rough
callused skin against silvery, satin
skin, his wet tongue coaxes
my nipples to stand, while his lips pull
my plump sex-flushed skin sucked
into a dark cave to be swirled
and twirled by the cool, hot, tip
of a tongue. I remember

to dwell in the positive. I promise
to exist in each sensation
and deposit it deep. Soon, I will dig

up each romantic memory when the negative
emotions hold my mind ransom, bind my mind's
intimate moments behind my back, tie them
into insignificant knots of fear, and plant them

in direct light. I refuse to remain blue. I want to remove
the aluminum from my soil, accept the beautiful light
shade of red and remember my chest in full bloom.

My Reflection In Black Satin

Yesterday,
the black satin
blackberry bush
imitated my angry
breasts. She gave up
her ample berries
bosoms. I mowed down
her bramble – flat.
I sliced it off
to the root. I'm jealous -
its berries recovered beautifully.

When A Sparrow Thinks Like An Eagle

The predator attacks
me. I attack back with fury
and boldness. I hop onto its back,
peck its head in a bid to defend
my life. I dig

my tiny sharp talons into its deep
red-brown feathers and drill its skull
relentlessly. I soar high,

the disease clings to my breasts
despite my valiant attempt
to shake it off. This stunning attack

lasts months. My predator gives-up,
soars away, it calls out in short,
raspy screams, *She won*. I lost

my breast,
yet remain
whole.

Pray & Push A Red Devil

My smooth frame fascinates him
as he navigates fingers across places
his lips mark with Xs & Os. He helps me
escape this new reality I have
been permanently sewn into.

I concentrate on my areola's softer side
of red. Inspect each mapped blue line,
a morning glory vein, beneath my skin
stitching through my breasts. I want
to be mended by the fisher of men. My God

voice begs me to understand
cancer, the size of a pencil tip, is deadly
as a beautiful angel's trumpet. I press

my upper biceps between my breasts,
press them flat. Instantly, I see a 13-year-old
chest, instead of a 49-year-old bouquet
of bosom. I pray for women

bound in pink ribbons. Peace
is found in the act of praying
and fasting, tucked inside Red
Devil cocktails, and dancing
through invisible gamma rays.

Sometimes tight threads must unravel.

Tequila Shots and Bullet Proof Vests

At high tide Sally arrives on a soapy back
of thick sea foam blooms, offers up Dos
Luna's, limes and a bounty of red spice
salts on the delicate quartz crystal
beach. A wealth of goddesses footsteps
crisscross. On the shores they dance
two-by-two. Hurricane Sally's musical notes,

second position to her text. Each word,
spiced with anger. A pinch reminds us,
too much bloodies our noses. We accepted the fall
season stretches its arms out for years,
brings changes to our bodies,
patterns of gold & orange bruises,
punctuated with long branches
of plastic noodle bulb drains. We were distorted,

yet fluid as fine India soot. We fill our wells
with pitch to pen our lives, on the quietest days
when our fingers need to hum. We drink
ourselves invisible. In minutes, our senses stir. The wind
cancels out, a concentration of sanity
flows between pink ladies. Their truth
is a bullet proof vest.

Meridian Road

I never obey imaginary boundaries
of longitude that measure the sunrise
and the sunset. The 90th meridian hides
under the black tar. This line tries to sturdy me,
and attempts to connect me to a home

base, my curiosity is never satisfied. I swerve
across the road's white shoulder lines. I search
for gratification directly on the broken yellow line. I gamble
on dull, gray skies and dive into tough, wild grass. I welcome
Texas blazing stars into the narrow space of my lower back. I
binge on the ripe blackberries who beg me to sample them. I feast,

return to a hot asphalt road, find the dry mud
mold of my feet, and I no longer fit. I never will
surrender to the thin imaginary line that measures.

Binding Wounds With Pink Ribbon

We four are learning to overcome
being gutted and stuffed survivors. At McGuire's
we begin with a Tiramisu martini, & steak dinner
with a side of waiter. Ultra-smooth air cleanses our lungs,
the dewy sea wind gently pushes us. We bow down

on knees to grass sentries surrounding
Golden Delicious apples. We cut
through, admire the loaded trees' plump fruits. Seductive
seedmen caress these fruit, heavily
blemished with bitter rot. They mirror
our corrupt images. We gently bind
pink ribbons around smooth bark. These trees

need to break their internal dams, release
gushing rivers from their trunks. They baptize the body
with acceptance. We all swallow apples whole,
slowly sip Anna apple cider and make plans
on how to shed our crumbling shell
and slip into a new creamy pink paper
skin scissored with two sharp white lines.

The orchard gardeners sing songs of fall hurricane
survivors, yet we ladies choose to rewrite love letters
upon our chests, become ascended masters
in the flesh and learn to enjoy gin and tonics
with a side of oxidated apples, dipped in dark chocolate.

EVOLUTION

My Body Bonded With Super Glue

I continue to move
slowly surveying his body
of land. A bird of prey has stolen
my treasured chest. It forces me to reflect,
survey the beauty of my upper torso. I make myself

park on top. His temperature rapidly intensifies. He whispers,
You are complete. His hands are the puzzle pieces that fit
into the space on my hard sternum. His empty hands continue
to steer me on this fast current of winds. Our bodies'
blood determines our arrival. We want to move
as pebbles in the stream. We cannot slow.
He is the only man I desire to ride with in
my traumatic thunderstorm, as it runs down
my empty chest. He predicts I will be unstoppable
because I steer directly into the winds,
my body tenses, until my involuntary release.

A Controlled Burn With a Twist of Lime

I'm deemed a rebel
without a cause. I no longer have a need
to place my feet into other people's shoes and travel
paths they forge. I use apple embers, entice a slow burn,
and limit all invasive species. Until I decide
to scorch the earth beneath their feet, heat their bodies,
and force them to release slowly and steadily. It is hard to control
this wild flame nature lights in my heart. This animal cannot always
be harnessed; it is also a welcome light that burns and warms. As I sip

my gin and tonic I realize I often hide the bitters in a mixture
of sugar, lime and fire waters and enjoy the citrus oils biting my lips.

Peeled Bark and Blushing Thighs

I love feeling my husband's skin
pressing against my empty chest,
as I push into his back. It entices us
to experiment. With each touch
pleasure is created. He understands

I want everything
reversed. I don't need a nurse,
I need a lover. His hands

a binding vine. We touch me
everywhere
as he concentrates on the weight
of his kisses against my shoulders,
abdomen, and thighs as I blush
a killer heat. It rounds my lips
and he transitions seamlessly,
underneath my frame. We nestle,

as I accept my bark is to be peeled
from my tender trunk.
I will enjoy the erotic
purple butterfly pea

flower and lime ice
between my lips. I miss the tingle
of the cool morning current
that implores my dead
two-inch circles to pop,
rise and come forth.

Cupping Coffee

Men love exotic, hidden treasures. They discover
passion in oysters and chardonnay. Their favorite
magazines reveal passionate messages: Hot

teas taste enticing with honey, while dripping
from a lover's tongue. Soft words
cause a body to throb. Every second
waits for the tongue and its desires to linger
on her pink pearl. She anticipates the touch. Gently
coax her fire to the surface, and when she glistens, she wants
to be taken and left whole. Between his lips,

he sips her bold, spice
coffee. Words roll
between her lips, she speaks not
of her scarred blank canvas. She learns

to lean over his cup,
she breaks its crust,
sticks her nose deep
into the coffee steam,
dips a silver spoon,
lifts it to a point
below her lip, and
sucks his warm brew
violently, into her
mouth. He smells of caramel,
bark, and chocolate. He is sharp,
burnt and fills her
abstract chest with warm.
He sweetens her bitter
taste with creamed honey.

Chasing Ghost in Corkscrew Swamp While Smoking Lemon Bean

He loves the thrill of hunting
for her. He hikes through knee-deep water
the color of sweet tea. He smokes palm leaves
filled with Lemon Bean. A euphoric spirit arouses him,
he must hunt a home steeped in mystery. Here, in a niche
in the deeper water swamp, under the large cypress
canopies, she is an elusive ghost

fairy, whose tendril fingers intertwine
her host. Whose lungs draw in
moisture air. In the shade, her home
of waterlogged trees, her mystery
deepens her lover's needs to touch,
and gaze upon her. God's artistry
has white lightning strikes that stand
out against a soft flesh void. Petals,
two delicate blossoms that flutter
in the breeze and hover. An open-top

dress entice these bare chest lovers to dance
the tango. He dips deep into his partner's
nectar. She feels the warmth of his flushed
cheeks between her thighs and is transported
to new worlds, pregnant with possibilities.

Thrilled by the Burn

She is chiseled from black liquid ink,
volcanic rock. She covers herself in a lush blanket
of silver words. Men's smooth adjectives
explode as they sink into her brown raisin
skin. She emits body heat, she melts. Droplets
of moisture drench her mossy surface
as she bathes in the firelight of the sunset. She stretches

vowels in high musical notes. These are
maps to her honey. A challenge coaxes men
to find her pulse, create an eruption. She breaks through
the earth's crust in the gold light of morning, her obscure
hexagon eyes search for her imaginary love,
and her puckered bee stung, suede
soft lips desire to taste his liquid blue
fin tongue. Passers-by sip her honey
wine nectar in a Bordeaux glass
filled with creamy cave pearls. She is
the woman who loves butter-
haired men running naked close to her
honeysuckle paths, straight into her
complexed, underground chambers.

Boys Who Wear White Enjoy Eating Red

She dares him to wear white
gloves while he eats her
red popsicle. She dares him to touch it,
his cheek against the plumpness
between her thighs. She dares him to rub
ruby stained lips against her
cherry bomb ammunition. He dares her to sip
a Red Devil martini. He dares her to drink
a liquid imaginary line. He dares her to dive
deep, show him her crinoline
of unforgettable loss. He dares her to bare
her beautiful void chest. On it he will write
words of desire. She dares him to whisper
while he slides fingers across her
scissored white lines. She dares him to knead her
skin. For dessert
he powders her body
with gold dust. He is a prize
stag. Her body, his
French mineral lick.

Life's Self Inflicted Performance

I sit silently in the proscenium box waiting for my scene
to begin. In a moment, under this bright house light,
my organs turn to liquid. My bright mind is gently soft
soaped by my Romeo. He enjoys the bite

into my warm layers hoping to find a hollow. He wants
to worm in my void. My pink, shiny wrapper attracts him
and he craves to slowly strip off my thickness,
crack my seal and taste the caramel

slowly oozing through my seams. He sometimes forgets
I am carved from granite. It is a gift via my father.
My mother's gift are words engraved on ribs: *Keep your eyes wide
shut when the moon hides the sun, but do not be afraid
when viewing the bright, bursting star.*

I sand rub these words off my bones, brush my body with oil,
sprinkle sugar, and brown my skin. On a stage,
lovers are baptized in honey and sea salt,
remove their hearts with a butter knife, bind

hands to feet and perform.

Amid A Body's Civil War

She brings a new meaning to the term *queen*
bee as she dances. An agreeable mob blankets her
body. A 12,000-bee necklace with a queen locket
surrounds her. She meditates, performs slow
movements, brimming with energy,
yet empty of sound. This tool heals. She no longer fears
her own bosom. She communes with silk,
arc-winged monsters, potential murders. They are sensual
while furious. She will not let cancer restrict her
movements. She leads the rise to dance. The routine

begins as she searches for life after cancer.
She is a queen that other women follow. As they land
into her world of a triple negative chest, they will
pinch, needing to hold fast to her positive energy,
her power is mixed with serenity. Her name
a constant buzz in everyone's ear.

An Ant's Exploration

I love when we play
pretend. You are comprised
of steep slopes. I am anxious

as an ant. My journey begins
across your body. In search of
the fragrance of your soul,
deep in your neck creases. A banquet
awaits me. I am curious and filled
with optimism as I survey your orchard,
finding the peaches hang robust, juicy
and sweet. Below this orchard,
a mossy garden, full of beauty.
Cascades of cherry blossoms. I yearn to pick
your pink flowers, steep them in tea,
and gorge myself on your bounty
until I am satisfied. I can't fight the urge

to feel the Devil seduce my tongue. The upper lip,
you allow me to lick. The bottom lip,
you allow me to bite.

Praise a Confident Woman

Delight in her
cockiness. She wears it
like the shine on her gold
bangle bracelets. Beautifully imperfect
chestnut meringue cakes
balance on her golden, engine-
oil skin, plump hips gently rest
open on beds of variegated Mana and Blue
Rush reeds. She offers lovers

desserts of her imperfect moon
pies filled with smooth cream
custard. Her lover lathers her
Fuji apple skin with
sugar. Butters and rolls her
in coarse sugar to taste
the winter and ice crystals
inside her cells.

Acknowledgements

"Girl in Chemise" received the Gwendolyn Brooks Emerging Writers' Award, 2015

I wish to thank my parents, Heurshel & Mildred "Net" Tellor, who taught me determination and introduced me to poetry. I am deeply appreciative of Beth Gordon for advising on this manuscript and believing in my voice. I also wish to thank my friends Kathy Galbraith, Kim Kurtak & Brenda Foschiatti for helping me shape parts of the narrative each year in Florida. I am also grateful to Deirdre Burnside for the cover art and for holding on to it for over 20 years. My love to my son Jeffery and my husband Jeff Sr. whose love and patience are unlimited and whose continued faith allows me to continue to grow as a poet.

About the Author

Lisa Tellor-Kelley won the 2015 State of Illinois Emerging Writer's Award. Previously, she was an English composition lecturer at Southern Illinois University Edwardsville, and a creative writing lecturer at Lindenwood University-Belleville, IL. Lisa is the name giver of the *River Bluff Review* literary journal at Southern Illinois University Edwardsville. Her poems have been published in *OVS-Organs of Voice & Speech*, *South Broadway Ghost Society*, *Assisi: Journal of Arts and Letters*, and *The River Bluff Review*. Currently, she spends her time writing poetry, indulging in rich food and drink while living in rural Southern Illinois.